its gonna hurt that boy
the second you get over him
-*its his loss*

i had forgotten how the sunlight felt against my skin. if i remembered then i might not be here. it made me want to crawl back in my car and hide. hide from reality. i like to believe id still be in bed counting down the minutes until i left my room if i wasnt here, but here i am standing outside of the therapists office with a tear falling from my cheek. i tried to distract myself.

is the sun really that unpleasant? i thought so, but then i dwelled on that thought for too long. deciding it wasnt the sunlight that was keeping me from leaving the house. it was the realization that i would have to do things without you. that i would have to talk about things, and how they ended. it was the fact that i would not be coming home to you anymore. this saddened me.

i finally built enough courage to open the door. the airconditioner felt nice and the lighting was dim. the air smelled like vanilla with just the right amount of warmth. as i sat in the waiting room my mind wandered on the questions i might get asked, and how i would respond to them.

will this actually help me? i thought. almost everyone i know has talked to a therapist at some point, but i never tried to pry in and ask them if it really truly helped. i cannot wrap my head around the thought of telling a stranger about losing my relationship, or the advice they might give me. the judgment that they will hide behind a nod.

but i need to do something
i cant sleep at night

thats the thing they dont tell you about manipulation
it molds itself into something
you mistake for love

the grief doesnt go away
the grief doesnt shrink
the grief stays

and we grow

you said we were somewhere inbetween
how could we ever be just friends
friends dont look at your lips
while youre talking to them

aliza grace

i hope you allow yourself to eat
when your body is hungry
i hope you sing and dance
to all your favorite songs
i hope you bought yourself
those flowers
the ones
he wouldnt
buy for you

take the little parts of me with you when you leave
remember my favorite songs
how we sung them together in your car
the words i whispered in your ear late at night
my coffee order
remember all of my secrets
keep them safe for me
wear my sweater
the one you took from my closet
remember how you taught me how to drive
the dream home we picked out together
on seventh street
my favorite food
these pieces of me will haunt you
but i hope they make you a better man
for the next girl

deep down you know
you know shes not me
you know that shes not
going to put up with you
like i did

you know deep down
she will never love you
the way i use to

her kiss will never
feel gentle and loving like mine
holding her hand will feel
like a chore

you will feel your heart
break inside of your chest
because shes not me

dont beg a boy to be a man
dont beg him to change
dont beg for flowers
dont beg for reassurance
dont beg him to post you
dont beg for a call back

dont beg for the bare minimum

aliza grace

i wish you knew
the feelings i have for you

i cant explain
the amount of love
i feel for you

i wish i could explain
the feeling i get when
i wake up beside of you

there is not any words
that fully encompass
how you make me feel

but i will start here
with i love you

not all people are meant to come into your life to stay. people come and go like seasons. but they are put in your life to serve a purpose. sometimes you only see the reason looking back. so when someone wants to leave. let them. they already served their purpose. soak up all of the valuable lessons you are taught along the way. pay close attention to the people who have stayed. the people who learned from you. your friends. the ones who grew with you.

aliza grace

when im with you
my mind goes blank
every little problem disappears
and for the first time
i feel at peace

this is how you know he is the one

you cant hate yourself
into someone you love
so take the time
put in the effort
learn to love
yourself

even if he hurts me
i still love him
my heart is forgiving
i cant say im always
proud of that
but i do know
that nothing he does
will ever take away
the memories
and all the reasons
i love him
all of me hopes
he sees this part of me
so soft and forgiving
maybe then he will
hold me closer and
protect me

you are mine now. i cannot imagine a happy fulfilling life without you. part of that may be my fault. perhaps its because i have already planned our wedding in my head. picked out the names for our future children. or because i know the house we dont have yet like the back of my hand. but dont confuse our love to a figment of my imagination. i simply cannot process a future where you are not mine.

im told i will look back on these days with a
grateful heart
that i will be happy i made it through
and while that seems to ease my stress
my stomach still sinks
i dont know what tomorrow holds
i dont know what the future is full of
but i hope and i pray
you are there with me

sometimes i feel like the book
the one that sits in the back of your closet
you read the first page
but something else caught your attention
distracting you from the plot
you were left missing out
on what could have been

my heart hurts for all of the women who have to check their spouses phone. i too know your pain. when he is asleep you reach for it. with every snore you dig deeper. finding out what was going on outside of your presence. your stomach will sink. this feeling along with what you find will haunt you. maybe even change you. your body will feel like its rotting beside of the person you thought you knew.

aliza grace

it hurts doesn't it?
seeing other boyfriends
do big romantic gestures
for their girlfriends

knowing he would never do that for you

existing with your absence
it is such an indescribable feeling
sometimes it makes me laugh
because there is no one
here to criticize me
i want to feel free
other times it makes me cry
because even your criticism
made me a better person
then i miss you

do you realize now
i was never the problem
the problem was
your lack of commitment
the problem was never me
because i am enough
the problem was you
because you
didnt see that

straight jeans
the smell of cigarettes
maybe you know me better then i do
the way i lost myself in your eyes
counting all of the lies you told
the way you could
get yourself out
of any situation

a week never felt that long
until i spent it without you
a month never felt that long
until i spent it without you

aliza grace

sometimes you have to walk away hurt
without hurting the other person
in time this will heal you
more than hurting them would

aliza grace

putting aside time for yourself is essential
you were beautifully fearfully made human
so when your body is tired listen to it
care for your souls dwelling
at the end of the day
its all you have

aliza grace

true love is when he
goes into the store
bringing you back
your favorite snack
even though you never
asked for it

i washed the sheets
the ones we shared
the sheets we slept tangled in
although now
i think i should
throw them away
because washing away
your scent
it doesnt wash away
the years of memories

nostalgia of your first breakup
you were young and he was dumb. he was the guy who gave you the least bit of attention. but that was enough for you. or so you thought. you lost yourself in big eyes and watered down lies. before you knew it you lost every worthwhile part of yourself to someone who didnt even know your birthday. i never believed all of the people who said girls mature faster then boys until i started dating.

aliza grace

when he left you shut all your emotions off
you didn't want to feel anything
and that seemed to work for awhile

the memories seemed to always linger
you let them in one too many times
convincing yourself this human was your person

but deep down you don't miss him anymore
you miss the potential
having someone to go to when something important
happens
a shoulder to ugly cry on
the person you showed your truest self to

he isn't here anymore

aliza grace

you don't post pictures of me on social media
you say something along the lines of

> *"i don't post on instagram anymore"*
"i don't use facebook"
> *"its not even that important"*

and its not
its not important to <u>you</u>
i just want to be shown off
i want people to know im your girl

> *is that too much to ask*

tell me your deepest fears
what kind of career you dreamed about as a child
when you first felt sadness
how you take your coffee
the happiest memories you have had
everything that means something to you
whatever you hold closest to your heart
i want to know every detail about you
ill fall in love with you over and over
each day

aliza grace

im not the girl
who catches your attention
in a room full of people

but he makes me feel seen

i want to be the love that doesnt make you forget
your saddest days
instead
i want to be the love that helps you to understand
they happen for a reason
one of the reasons being
you have these sad bitter days
so you know
you really know the happy ones

im sorry you have gotten hurt in the past
im sorry for all the trauma they gave you
im sorry for all the insecurities they gave you
im sorry you got cheated on
im sorry they made you think that you are unlovable

the apology that you deserve

aliza grace

each day feels the same
i do the same things
and i just cant break the cycle
feeling so alone in a room full of people
staying up till the next morning then falling asleep
when its bright outside
this isn't a life
and i don't know what im doing
i want to take care of myself
the weight of getting out of bed to comb my hair
just feels too heavy for me right now
im normally a clean and organized person
but there are dishes and dirty clothes all over my
room

is this what depression feels like

aliza grace

why is letting go so hard
after all the pain you put me through
after all the tears shed
because of you

we were all each other had most nights

aliza grace

it was you
that made me feel whole
even when i was never sure
half of me was there

aliza grace

before begging him to change
would you leave if he didnt

the reason i kept going back to him
knowing he would keep hurting me
was because i wanted to feel nothing for him
i wanted him to hurt me so bad
i would never think about going back again
and thats what happened

the pain he inflicted
it stays in your bones
it becomes part of you
you learn to live with it
and one day
it will be the reason
you gain
enough courage
to leave

aliza grace

here you are
after everything
you endured
he left you
heartbroken
and walked
away in one
piece

aliza grace

i loved you more
then i have ever tried
to love myself

you walk away like i mean nothing to you. i wish we could trade hearts. only then i could feel nothing for you. the way you feel nothing for me. you make being emotionless look so easy.

aliza grace

what do you see when you look at me now
do you see a girl who broke herself
loving a man who never even acknowledged
the amount of love she gave him

aliza grace

the heartbreak will consume you
leave you on a tear soaked pillow
take away your appetite for weeks
you'll start to hate the way you look
you dye your hair a darker shade
mascara will be on your cheeks
you will take a moment to process everything
and even in this state of your life
you wouldn't have had it any other way
even in your weakest moments now
it was worth it to you
all because you once had him

your so excited for the future
while i relate to that
take a breath
enjoy the now
you will never have
the past
all you have is now

aliza grace

you can do anything you want to
right now
not in memories
or the past
only now

                          with that being said
              make memories you want to remember
                    dance with people you love
                          and tell them all
                          how you feel
                          before its too late

aliza grace

being woman is a form of art
look how beautiful
you were made
without comparing yourself

you can miss him
without begging for him back
you can cry for him
without going back to him

healing

if you could ask him one question
what would you ask?
i dont stutter or hesitate. instead my mind races to
all of the questions i have left unanswered.
"why did you leave?"
"was i not good enough?"
"how long did you think about leaving?"
"did you know it was the last time you would see
me?"
"do you miss me?"
"do you miss us?"
    -   and the list goes on

you cant
love someone
into loving you back

what i need you to realize

it might take days or months
but you will feel inspired again

loving him is easy. i feel safe in his presence. and he doesnt flinch when i grab his phone. loving him makes me want to better myself. i want to grow together. loving him makes me feel beautiful. something that has been so foreign to me. he showers me in compliments and kisses. he doesnt make me feel bad for saying no. i feel most myself with him anyways. being with him has taught me so much. finally experiencing a healthy relationship has allowed me so much happiness. so yes loving him is easy.

you left and i questioned myself
i questioned what love was
and i left that thought floating in my mind
to dwell on for winter
until the snow melted and tulips bloomed
it hit me like a brick in the face
i don't know what love is
but i know its something
you never gave me

aliza grace

not sure who needs to hear this
but you cant change him

aliza grace

you will heal
i promise
               or with time
        you will be able to
           live with it
                         heal when you
                         are truly ready
                            not when
                     they say you should

maybe the depression lingers
wanting to be seen
just like all of us
perhaps once you see it
you can humanize it
and overcome it

setting yourself free

to whatever soul
that mentioned to me
if you cant sleep at night
its because
your in someones dream
i hope you are right
i hope im in his

im still learning each day how to love myself despite being poisoned not to. corporations dont want us to love ourselves. because if we did then who would they sell there chemicals to.

aliza grace

nothing feels more intimate
than being understood

you will know it is love. you will never have to ask twice. it wont feel like a chore to be present with them. instead you find comfort in their presence. being with them heals your inner child. you will know it is love when they never ask for more or less. because you are already enough. when its midnight and they lay awake stroking your hair because your peace means more to them then rest. you will know it is love because when you ask for reassurance they are never mad.

an apology goes out to all the hearts
i have broken
the people i let down
the things i did to you
i have felt myself
the universe sometimes has painful
ways of teaching us love

aliza grace

he knew how to love me with words
but his actions always said different

aliza grace

one of the scariest things
i have realized
is its up to you
to save yourself

on my lowest days
i think about the love we once shared
the days that we only had each other

i think about you
and how i hope you found it
whatever it was that took you away from me
i hope it makes your soul happy

i hope the best for you after all

aliza grace

you never had any intentions
on loving me back

no one said breakups are easy
thats because they aren't
going through a breakup hurts
it will have you on the bathroom floor sobbing
you will lose your appetite
your favorite foods wont taste the same
your bed will be your favorite place for a couple
weeks

but

its not always going to be this hard
and im not just saying that
with time it will get easier
it wont go away but you will be able to live with it
days and nights will fade into months
and he wont be the first thing you think about when
you first wake up anymore
i hope you can find comfort in that

i dont want to forget. i want to be okay with remembering. i dont want what we had to fade into nothingness. i want to be grateful of the time we had together.

but im still full of anger

you think you have replaced me
but you will soon realize
how irreplaceable i am
how no other girl
is going to love you
how i once did
and this will sadden you
because you will never
be able to find me
in another soul
you will be left
with memories
and my past

aliza grace

love was meeting you
and knowing from that moment on
it was you i wanted
each day forward

aliza grace

you torture yourself stalking her instagram
you know what you're doing
you just cant stop

comparing yourself

aliza grace

a conversation about how you feel
is not suppose to end in an argument

aliza grace

never let the same person
pretend to love you twice

aliza grace

"do you miss me"

each night before i fall asleep
i think about you
you are my first thought in the morning time
i cant get you out of my mind

"no"

aliza grace

she gets so upset about you
liking other girls pictures
because she sees which guys like her pictures
when its someones boyfriend
she thinks about how stupid he is making her look

how to let go

step 1 remember its okay to out grow people, places, and things. its okay for them to outgrow you too.

step 2 allow yourself to grieve the loss of what you're letting go of. you can never heal what you don't feel.

step 3 ask yourself if what you are holding onto is also holding on to you. answer honestly.

step 4 forgive yourself for your part in how things ended, just like how you forgave them for the unforgivable countless times.

step 5 remember relationships don't have to last forever to have meaning in our life.

step 6 sometimes the only closure you get is accepting the past cant change. and that is okay.

step 7 letting go is letting in. making room for something new is hard but worth it.

to the person reading this right now i hope that you are choosing yourself. i know you have been dealt a great deal of heartbreak. i know you have been let down too many times to count. so much that you have convinced yourself love isn't real. let me reassure you love is real. i am absolutely sure of that. you should be too. sometimes love isn't mutual and that is where it fools us.

i never believed in love
until i seen the way i loved him.

sometimes people come into your life and you know they will leave an impact on you. they creep in when you least expect it. they find you when your guard is down. and for a second everything feels right. you understand each other. it feels refreshing to be heard. it feels nice listening to what they have to say.

show her you care. yes. she is yours right now. but look at her. her eyes are full of galaxies and she smiles as soon as she sees you. she is not the type of girl you get to love twice. do it right the first time. buy her the flowers. stop beside the road and hand pick her flowers. she is well worth the effort. that girl would do anything for you. she has always put you first. you say shes your world but your actions say otherwise.

i wish i could give you the world. but i cant. so instead i will give you my heart. and enough love to fill it in this lifetime. i will give you my hand to hold and my lips to kiss.

aliza grace

stop trying
to prove your worth
to people who
were never deserving
of knowing you

aliza grace

a little reminder
you are allowed
to talk about
what they did to you
and how it hurt you
it does not matter
how they feel
about you talking about it
because if they wanted people
to think better of them
they should have been better

aliza grace

sometimes bad people
teach us lessons
they show their true colors
at the right time
and sometimes that
in itself leads us
in the right direction

aliza grace

if he makes sense to you
dont let anyone
talk you out of it

aliza grace

he looked the way
that honey tasted
sweet and earthy

he makes me feel
the same way music does

aliza grace

all of my relationships before you
were lessons on what love isnt

love isnt the voice in your head
begging you to leave him

love isnt leaving you awake
crying all night long

love isnt someone who leaves
when you need them most

you said he felt like home
people arent homes
they are ever changing beings
even when he radiates love
when his love for you
lights up the whole room
just know that can change
in any given instance
that feeling can burn out
and never come back
its quite unfair but there
is nothing you can do
but sit back and watch the boy
you fell for give up on you
this isnt the feeling i want you
to confuse home with

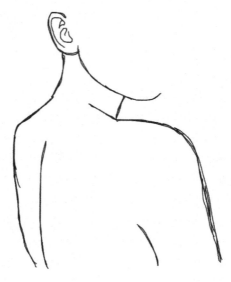

no one said it was easy
relationships are not easy
breakups are not easy
waking up everyday
choosing to love you
is not easy
this is not a film
we are people with real emotions
with indescribable feelings about each other
nothing in life is ever easy
love is not easy
but trust me its worth it

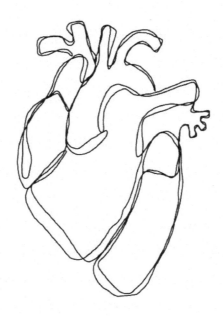

you convince yourself that you are over him. but if you were really over him would his name still be in your search history. would his favorite songs still be on repeat. you are still wearing his hoodie to bed. deep down you still love him. the truth is you dont know how to stop.

im proud of you for taking the long way. the hard road. im proud of you for still standing strong on your opinions despite the hate. im proud of you for growing as a person this year. im proud of you for accepting what cannot change.

im so proud of you

> *i hope you are proud too*

aliza grace

i think its okay to keep your distance
its okay to be silent for awhile
there is importance in taking the time
you need to gather your words
sometimes things just need to sink in

you cant change what happened
the past is not reversible
but the future has not been made yet
learn from your mistakes
better times are coming

there is no good reason
to ever lie to me
i am a understanding person
the only thing i deserve
is the truth

i always told you the truth even when it was ugly

aliza grace

whatever you are going through
it isn't a reflection of yourself
never compare your value
to rough waters

aliza grace

you are more than your body
dont let the scale trap you
in such a negative headspace
we are humans
who live everyday
on a floating rock
in outer space
you have the capacity
to do anything you want
yet you are so
obsessed with your weight

aliza grace

i deleted your number
i deleted the messages
i deleted the pictures
i blocked you
i felt nothing

her love will feel forced. it will never flow through her lips on to yours the same way mine did. her back will not curve at your touch. our names sound completely different. yet i hear you confuse them often. somedays i question if she is even your type. but something tells me you wanted someone different. someone to help you forget me.

healing is not easy
forgetting you is impossible
everyday i am learning
how to give up pieces of you
and one day there just
wont be any left

forcing myself to unlove you

you leave him
before you get left
you want love
but you are afraid
of getting hurt

i want to see
the real you
when you are tired
after a long day at work
i want to see you
when you are most yourself

aliza grace

i never wanted an apology
i wanted change
an apology without change
is manipulation

aliza grace

hurts me 217 times

*maybe i should give them
a second chance*

aliza grace

the ugly truth
there is no
right person
wrong time

he didnt break you. sure. it hurt went he left. but he didnt break you. he taught you plenty of valuable lessons. people who walk away so easy were never deserving of you. let them go. he taught you what you deserve. and as bad as you wanted it to be him. its not.

dont be afraid to lose people
if you lose them so easy
were they ever worth having around

the smell of your cologne
is tattooed on my mind
your big brown forgive me eyes
i can never resist
how it felt
the first time
we shared a kiss
there are a million
things i love
about you

aliza grace

first loves teach us
what love isn't

aliza grace

how was i suppose to know
i would end up alone
when you promised me forever
and sealed it with a kiss
i believed you

aliza grace

its not your fault
you had so much love
for someone
who hurt you so bad
and it also isn't your loss
its theirs

aliza grace

its okay to make mistakes
you are not broken
things will get better
you deserve the purest
truest unconditional love
dont settle for less

aliza grace

as long as i am breathing
you will always be loved

aliza grace

defend her in public
correct her in private

healing doesnt happen overnight
missing him comes in waves
first its deleting old pictures
then before you know it
hes blocked
healing
doesnt happen
all at once

aliza grace

you deserve
the same love you give

you are more than enough
i am sorry he didnt realize that

aliza grace

i
miss
the
warmth
of
your
voice

signs someone is good for you
after you spend the day together you feel a sense of peace
you can be your most authentic self around them
they fully support you and what you want to do
they never put you down or hold you back

you must be okay
with your past
in order to focus
on whats in front
of you

you did it
despite everything
that was ever in your way
you climbed the mountain
overcame more than anyone
ever asked you to
so enjoy the view